WINSTER : a Souvenir Guide.

by

JOHN N. MERRILL

PHOTOGRAPHS   AND   MAP   BY   JOHN N. MERRILL

a J.N.M. PUBLICATION

1989

a J.N.M. PUBLICATION

JNM PUBLICATIONS,
WINSTER,
MATLOCK,
DERBYSHIRE.
DE4 2DQ

This book is copyright under the Berne Convention. All rights are reserved. Apart from any fair dealing for the purposes of private study, research, criticism or review, as permitted under the Copyright Act, 1956, no part of this publication may be reproduced, stored in a retrieval system, or transmitted in any other form by any means, electronic, electrical, chemical, mechanical, optical, photocopying, recording or otherwise, without the prior permission of the copyright owner. Enquiries should be addressed to the publishers.

Conceived, edited, typeset, designed, marketed and distributed by John N. Merrill.

© Text and route — John N. Merrill 1989

© Map and photographs — John N. Merrill 1989

First Published — January 1977
Reprinted 1985
This enlarged edition — March 1989

ISBN 0 907496 81 4

Meticulous research has been undertaken to ensure that this publication is highly accurate at the time of going to press. The publishers, however, cannot be held responsible for alterations, errors or omissions, but they would welcome notification of such for future editions.

Printed by:

Set in Baskerville — Roman, Italic and Bold.

Sketches by John Creber. © JNM Publications — Front Cover — Winster Market House. Back Cover — Winster Hall Inn Sign.

ABOUT JOHN N. MERRILL

John combines the characteristics and strength of a mountain climber with the stamina and athletic capabilities of a marathon runner. In this respect he is unique and has to his credit a whole string of remarkable long walks. He is without question the world's leading marathon walker.

Over the last fifteen years he has walked more than 100,000 miles and successfully completed ten walks of at least 1,000 miles or more.

His six major walks in Great Britain are -
Hebridean Journey .... 1,003 miles
Northern Isles Journey .... 913 miles
Irish Island Journey .... 1,578 miles
Parkland Journey .... 2,043 miles
Lands End to John o'Groats .... 1,608 miles
and in 1978 he became the first person (permanent Guinness Book of Records entry) to walk the entire coastline of Britain — 6,824 miles in ten months.

In Europe he has walked across Austria — 712 miles — hiked the Tour of Mont Blanc, completed High Level Routes in the Dolomites and Italian Alps, and the GR20 route across Corsica in training! In 1982 he walked across Europe — 2,806 miles in 107 days — crossing seven countries, the Swiss and French Alps and the complete Pyrennean chain — the hardest and longest mountain walk in Europe, with more than 600,000 feet of ascent!

In America he used the the world's longest footpath — The Appalachian Trail -2,200 miles — as a training walk. He has walked from Mexico to Canada via the Pacific Crest Trail in record time — 118 days for 2,700 miles. In Canada he has walked the Rideau Trail.

During the summer of 1984, John set off from Virginia Beach on the Atlantic coast, and walked 4,226 miles without a rest day, across the width of America to Santa Cruz and San Francisco on the Pacific Ocean. His walk is unquestionably his greatest achievement, being, in modern history, the longest, hardest crossing of the USA in the shortest time — under six months (178 days). The direct distance is 2,800 miles.

Between major walks John is out training in his own area — the Peak District National Park. As well as walking in other parts of Britain and Europe he has been trekking in the Himalayas five times. He has created more than ten challenge walks which have been used to raise more than 250,000 for charity. From his own walks he raised over 80,000. He is author of more than ninety books, most of which he publishes himself. His book sales are in excess of 2 million.

iii

CONTENTS

Page No

INTRODUCTION	1
BRIEF HISTORY	2
TWO-MILE WALK	⎫
MARKET HOUSE	⎬ 9
BANK HOUSE	⎪
WORKHOUSE	⎭
MINERS STANDARD	⎫
LEAD ORE HOUSE & MOSEY MERE	⎬ 11
ODDO HOUSE	⎪
PARISH CHURCH	⎭
DOWER HOUSE	⎫ 15
HALL	⎭
FOLKLORE	⎫ 17
MORRIS DANCING	⎭
PANCAKE RACES	17
WINSTER WAKES CAKE	18
OTHER BOOKS BY JOHN N. MERRILL	19

Morris Dancers — about 1952

iv

Winster People — partially ruined Market House behind — about 1900.

INTRODUCTION

Driving along the B5057 road from Darley Dale, you pass through the village of Darley Bridge before ascending to the limestone village of Wensley. As you do so, you enter the Peak District National Park. Through Wensley the road levels out, giving fine views across a wide wooded valley. Suddenly and quite dramatically you reach the village of Winster. As you reduce speed and enter the Main Street, you are immediately struck by the beauty and age of the houses. Most are 18th Century, with the Market House dating back to the 16th Century. Stop, don't continue your journey! Winster and its surroundng area is quite unique and well worth a couple of hours' perusal.

Winster's brief history is enumerated on the forthcoming pages. By completing a two-mile walk through the village and surrounding area you will be able to see at first hand many features of interest in the Winster story. It is a fascinating story, and I hope you enjoy your visit.

JOHN N. MERRILL
Winster.

BRIEF HISTORY

At the time of the Domesday Book, Winster is named — Winsterne, meaning Wine'sthryne (thorn bushes). The entry describes the village as being — "two districts, each with a residence, occupied by Lewing and Raven. About 12 acres of land for tax. Cola, the agent of Henry de Ferrers, managed seven small farmers. 12 cottages held a small plot of land each. Between them they worked four ploughs. There was a wood half a mile wide and deep. Rateable value — One pound." A Norman chapel was built in the late 11th Century and stood on the site of the present church. The 16th Century Dower House adjacent to the church is believed to be on the site of the Manor Houses.

Little is known about Winster until the 17th Century. The village, which is part of the High Peak Hundred, was at the time of the Domesday Book owned by Henry de Ferrers, who later became the first Earl of Derby. His manors, which totalled 114 in Derbyshire, were later confiscated. In Henry the Third's reign the Earl of Lancaster was in possession of Winster; later it belonged to the Mountjoys, then the Blouts, Meynells, and during Elizabeth the First's reign the freeholders purchased it. It was during her reign that a significant change was heralded over the village and Peak District. In 1596 she granted that the old trade of lead mining be restored. In time Winster became a boom town, which accounts for the many 18th Century buildings in the village. More than sixty are listed buildings, and the village is now a conservation area.

In 1577, following a census of tavern owners in Derbyshire, Winster was found to have "no taverns, inn or alehouse". Lead mining appears to have been done on a family business scale during the 17th Century. The Hall was built in 1628 by Francis Moore, and a later member of the family became the barmaster. He was a representative of the Crown and responsible for the administration of mining law.

In 1676 the population of Winster was about 600. The majority lived around the Market Hall area of the village, but another smaller village existed to the west of the Miners Standard Inn, known as Islington, close to the rich Portway veins. By the beginning of the 19th Century this village had gone, and today the lane — Islington Lane — forming part of the Portway, reminds us of this last settlement. The Portway is an Anglo-Saxon name for a major highway. It is originally believed to have run from Nottingham along the eastern side of the Peak District.

By the early 18th Century many of the lead mines in the area were flooded, making mining a very awkward and expensive exercise. Two developments at this time — the smelting of lead using a cupola, and a fire engine, the Newcomen Atmospheric Engine, for pumping out the water — brought about a revolution, lifting the industry out of the doldrums into a booming one of which the present architecture of Winster bears ample evidence.

The London Lead Company became highly involved in lead mining in the Winster area and poured a small

West Bank — Shoulder of Mutton on right

fortune into the mines. By 1733 they had five fire engines working. Portway Mine, which is known to have been worked as far back as 1666, was one of the richest mines in Derbyshire. Between the years October 1746 to December 1753, more than 31,850 loads of lead ore were produced, selling for £63,718. In 1789, during the space of seven weeks when a particularly rich vein was found, the mine made a profit of £4,000. Placket Mine was another prosperous mine, and in 1763 a profit of £7,750 was made. According to legend, the engine boiler blew up, stopping the pumping and resulting in the mine closing down. Lying between West and East Bank is the mound of Orchard Mine. In the Winster area there were more than twenty lead mines operating in the 18th Century, and six soughs for draining them. The cost of the soughs was enormous. Yatestoop Sough was started in 1743 and finished in 1764 at a cost of more than £30,000 for its 2½ mile length.

All this work and prosperity brought about a complete change in the village. For the fifty years between 1720-1770, Winster grew rapidly in size with a population of well in excess of 2,000 and with more than twenty inns. Virtually all the houses you see were built during this period and are the result of the high wages and profits from the mines. The latter half of the 18th Century saw the price of lead decline, resulting in mining being barely a profitable business, especially when the costs of draining and pumping were so high. As a result work ceased, and only one or two continued working until the beginning of the 19th Century. Ferber, when he visited Winster in 1770, noted that most of the mines were 'overflowed'. Viscount Torrington visited Winster in 1790 and wrote — "all the county is scooped with lead mines, and their levels; betwixt Winster and Elton are the great lead mines of Port-way". He also wrote, Winster was a "much better and gayer place than Bakewell".

The decline of the industry is reflected in the population figures. In 1761 the population was 1,563, and within the previous eight years six inns had closed, leaving only eighteen. Today there are only three! In 1789 many of the houses on the main street were unoccupied, and the population was just over 1,000. Twenty years later in 1801 it was 753, a figure very similar to today's. J. Aikin in his book — "A Description of the Country from 30 to 40 miles around Manchester", published in June 1795 — writes about Winster:-

> "Winster is a market town containing 218 houses. The inhabitants chiefly depend upon lead mines for support. These having been for some time in declining state, the poor have employed themselves in picking and cleaning cotton for Sir Richard Arkwright's works."

Winster was renowned for its Markets, although there is no known Grant. Market Day was Saturday and was principally for butcher's meat. It was said that, "a peck of potatoes, a peck of meat and a pound of butter could be purchased for a shilling in Winster Market." A peck is a dry measure for goods and equals two gallons. Market Day was a scene of great activity, and Lewellan Jewitt wrote in the 19th Century (he lived at the Hall) — "Its market was so flourishing with long rows of stalls and the

East Bank — about 1890

people so thick and throng together you could a walk'd a top o' their heads." An earlier owner of the Hall, George Moore, wrote in his diary on July 8th 1778 — "I propose to go to Buxton today out of the way of the Market." Fairs too were a popular and major event on the calendar, but it is now more than a century since either were last held. Today, only the Wakes Week retains one of the old customs in late June each year. The annual pancake races, on Shrove Tuesday, are still held and are unique to Derbyshire. Winster is an ardent supporter of Morris Dancing, with its own team and dances.

Miners' Standard Inn sign

The Market House — 1989

Market House — about 1900 — notice Angel Hotel sign on left

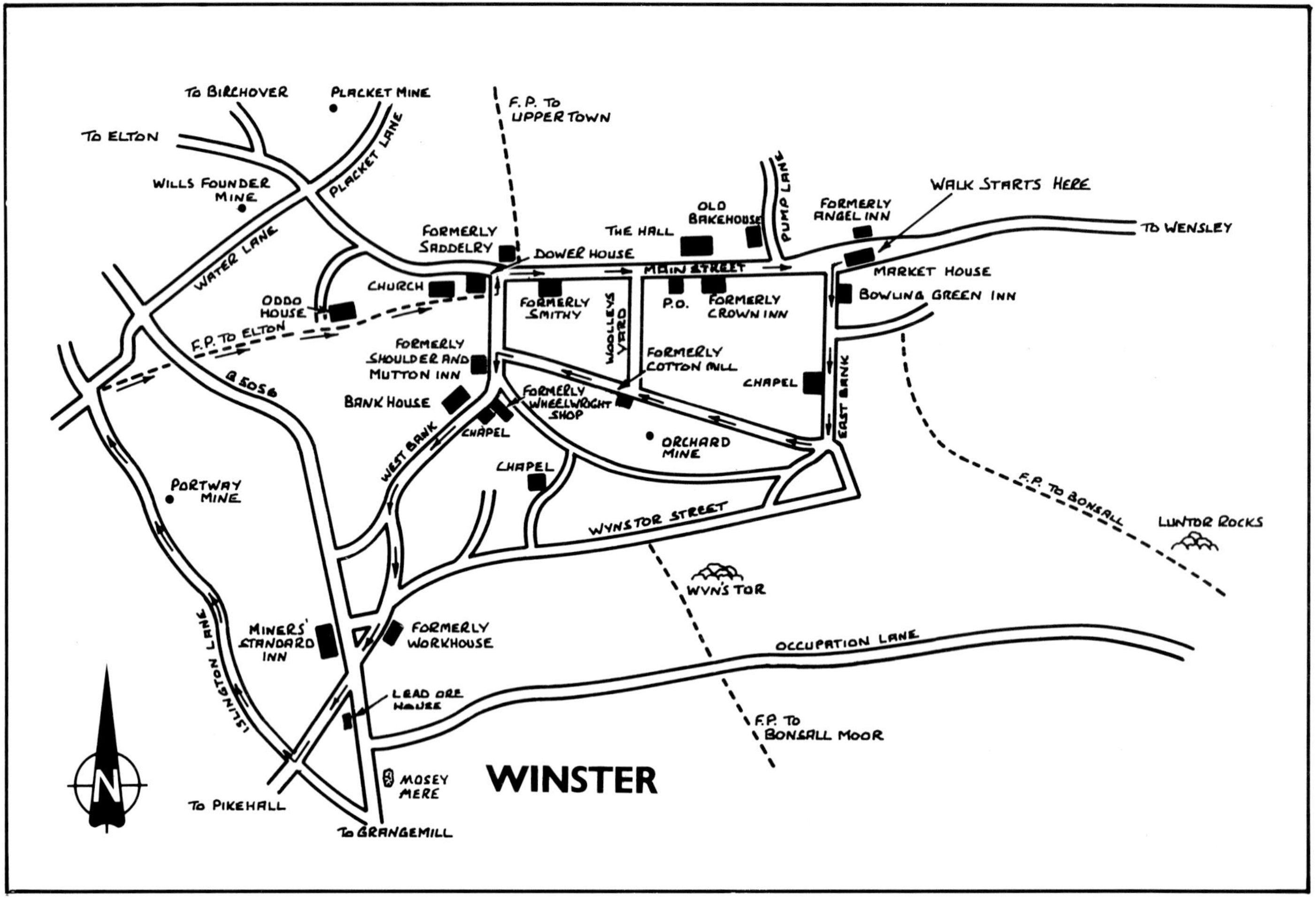
TO BIRCHOVER
PLACKET MINE
F.P. TO UPPER TOWN
TO ELTON
WILLS FOUNDER MINE
PLACKET LANE
WATER LANE
PUMP LANE
OLD BAKEHOUSE
FORMERLY ANGEL INN
WALK STARTS HERE
TO WENSLEY
THE HALL
FORMERLY SADDELRY
DOWER HOUSE
MAIN STREET
MARKET HOUSE
CHURCH
BOWLING GREEN INN
ODDO HOUSE
FORMERLY SMITHY
WOOLLEYS YARD
P.O.
FORMERLY CROWN INN
F.P. TO ELTON
FORMERLY SHOULDER AND MUTTON INN
FORMERLY COTTON MILL
CHAPEL
EAST BANK
B 5056
BANK HOUSE
FORMERLY WHEELWRIGHT SHOP
CHAPEL
WEST BANK
ORCHARD MINE
CHAPEL
PORTWAY MINE
F.P. TO BONSALL
LUNTOR ROCKS
WYNSTOR STREET
WYN'S TOR
MINERS' STANDARD INN
FORMERLY WORKHOUSE
OCCUPATION LANE
ISLINGTON LANE
LEAD ORE HOUSE
F.P. TO BONSALL MOOR
N
MOSEY MERE
WINSTER
TO PIKEHALL
TO GRANGEMILL

TWO MILE WALK

The following walk from the Market House in the Main Street brings you to many of the places mentioned in the brief history, to others described in the walk text and to those detailed on the map.

MARKET HOUSE — Two storeys high and standing in the Main Street. The lower storey of thick gritstone blocks is 16th Century. Originally the five filled-in arches would have been open, in common with usual market house design. The upper storey is 18th Century and probably replaces a timber construction. By the end of the last century the house was in a decaying state. It was given to the National Trust in 1906, becoming the first Trust property in Derbyshire. The upper storey was rebuilt using the original materials where possible, and cost £165. The building now serves as a National Trust Information Centre and shop, and is open to the public during the summer months on Wednesday, Saturday and Sunday afternoons — 2 p.m. to 6 p.m.

From the Market House, turn left up East Bank, passing the Bowling Green Inn on your left and later a Wesleyan Chapel dated 1823 on your right. A little past the chapel, turn right along a 'gennel', giving excellent views of the village as you walk past the top of Woolley's Yard to West Bank. As you do so you pass the mound of Orchard Mine on your left. Notice too the splendid architecture of the houses on East Bank and Woolley's Yard. At West Bank turn left and ascend the road past the former Shoulder of Mutton Inn and Wheelwright Shop, Bank House and the former Workhouse near the minor road (B5056) and close to the Miners' Standard Inn.

WHEELWRIGHT SHOP — Now known as Yew Cottage, the home of J.N.M. Publications. Believed to have been built in 1760. The earliest known deeds date from 1847, when the cottage and cowhouse were sold for £150 to George Henstock, a wheelwright. The house opposite, built at the beginning of this century, is on the site of another wheelwright shop.

BANK HOUSE — Built about 1580. A plaque on the right-hand side of the doorway records that the house has been the home of the village doctor for more than 100 years. The lawn outside the front door was once the scene of a murder. On Tuesday May 22nd 1821, William Cuddie, the surgeon and apothecary of Winster, was murdered by William Brittlebank of Oddo. For a while there was a reward of £100 for the capture of Brittlebank, who was 27 years old and 5 ft. 8 ins. tall. Naturally, he had vanished. William Cuddie's tombstone can be seen in the churchyard and is on the right-hand side of the pair of trees, forming an arch over the path when approached from West Bank.

WORKHOUSE — The workhouse was established in 1744, and had nine rules for the management of the occupiers. The seventh rule — When any of the poor be employed out of the house, the Overseer shall take the benefit of their work for their better maintenance and relief. John Johnson was appointed in charge of the

Lead Ore House

Photo shows second ODDO HOUSE

Mosey Mere

Church about 1920

10

Workhouse in 1744 for the salary of d10 per annum. Two entries from the Overseer's Accounts — April 18th 1752 — 1 child's coffin — 2/6d (12 p). October 28th 1765 — 3.10s. (3.50) — for 28 weeks of milk.

MINERS' STANDARD INN — The name is almost the only reminder of the once prolific lead mining industry in the area. The inn was built in 1653, and over the doorway can be seen the date and the initials E.P.; E.P.; F.P. They stand for Edith, Ella and Frank Prince — although they were often said to mean, cEvery person entering pays for a pint!

LEAD ORE HOUSE — A former lead ore nightsafe. Used by lead miners upton 50 years ago. The lead was deposited down a chute and the building is particularly strong having a vaulted roof.

MOSEY MERE — Just a little further up the road on the lefthand side is this mere. Water does not usually lie on the surface in limestone country but here it is covered with volcanic rock and the water cannot seep through. The water was used by the village of Islington.

Cross the road (B5056) to the left of the inn and walk along the road signposted for Newhaven, just ahead on your right is the Lead Ore House and further to the left is Mosey Mere; both worth exploring before continuing the walk. After approximately 75 yards, turn right down a walled lane, known as Islington Lane. As you walk down you pass close to the site of Islington Village on your left and Portway Mine on your right. After half a mile, at the junction of a farm road on your left, turn right as footpath-signposted and walk across the fields to the B5056 road. Cross to the stile and follow the path past Oddo House and into the churchyard. As you do so, look to your left. You are in limestone country, but scarcely a mile away is gritstone country and the outcrops of Cratcliffe and Robin Hood's Stride.

ODDO HOUSE — This is the third house to occupy this site. Oddo is associated with the Brittlebank family, who first came to Winster in 1700 when Hugh Brittlebank, an assistant Solicitor, and his wife moved there. A later Brittlebank became renowned for the murder he committed in 1821 on the lawn of Bank House. The Brittlebanks left Oddo in 1891. Their house was described as a bmodern residence erected in substantial manner, regardless of cost.c They also owned a considerable amount of the village, and together with the house were sold 3 farms, 68 'lots' choice accommodation' and 'meadow and pasture land'. The total area was 273 acres, 2 roods and a perch. The walk through Oddo to the church is particularly attractive, and grey squirrels are frequently seen in the trees close to the churchyard.

CHURCH — Dedicated to St. John the Baptist. Winster was formerly one of five chapelries connected to Youlgreave. In 1650 the Parliamentary Commissioner suggested that Elton and Winster be united into one parish. Today both are individual parishes but the living combines both, with the vicar living in Winster. The church, apart from the tower which was built in 1721, was rebuilt

Painting of Church — 1870

and enlarged in 1842 at a cost of about 1,600. In 1883 it was enlarged again, and is the present building we see here today. The interior has two aisles with three thin quatrefoil shafts in the middle. They are surprisingly thin, but in keeping. The one nearest the chancel joins the chancel arch by means of two arches. The font has always been regarded with curiosity, and its date is uncertain. Pevsner states that it could be a Tudor imitation of Norman workmanship. The clock was fitted in 1846 and cost d80.

From the Church Accounts, which make interesting reading, we learn that the five bells were brought to the church at a cost of 20.16s.9d.(20.83p). They were hung by Jacob Holmes for a cost of 3.8s.0d.(3.40p). The bell ropes cost 7 shillings (35p). During the 18th Century there was a permanent mole catcher, and in 1737 he received 3 a year for the service. Whilst many children died very young — four months, eight months and thirteen months old, for instance — many people lived to great ages. One woman, Ann Hawley, died on 8th March 1661, above 100 years oldc. The oldest man, John Rains, was buried on December 13th 1881, aged 97 years. Another member of the Rains family was Joseph Rains, who was buried on November 4th 1866, aged 62. A notice at the rear of the Burial Register records the event.

Found dead in River Derwent, November 3rd. Verdict - Accidental death. He was a well-known character in the village — thoroughly clean and honest — for many years was a servant of the late Andrew Brittlebank Esq., and was often entrusted by him with large sums of money, all of which, though he was frequently intoxicated, he brought

safely (he is known to have hidden it in his shoe and to have walked from the Bank at Wirksworth with it in that position). On Sunday October 21st, he went to Matlock and was never seen alive again — and though every means

was used and no expense was spared to recover the body, all efforts failed — until November 3rd. The body was seen floating quietly down the stream of the River Derwent

at Matlock. He is supposed to have attempted to return to Winster at night by the foot-road along the meadows from Matlock Bridge (where he was last seen) and to have missed his footing and fallen into the river.

Another entry records — Catherine Orme — buried Feb. 10th 1866,
aged 39. Found dead — Feb. 7th — having hung herself from
the house beam. Verdict of the Jury — Temporary insanity.

Another — 1874 — Kathleen Mary Higgins. Buried Jan. 21st, aged 16 months. Died from sucking 'lucifer matches'.

There are many entries of deaths down the lead mines and of persons falling down shafts, such as bAnthony Hardy, came to his death by falling down a shaft at a mine called Mill Close within the liberty of Wensley in the

13

Winster Hall

Parish of Darley 19th July 1823, aged 15 years.c

1870 — Joseph Beardow — Buried Sept. 18th 1870, aged 46. Crushed to death by a wheel (water wheel) at Ecclestor Mine at 4 o'clock in the afternoon of Thursday, September 15th.

From the churchyard, walk past the walls of the Dower House onto West Bank. Turn left, shortly before turning right and walking along the Main Street back to the Market House. As you do so you see the Dower House, the 18th Century three-storey-high buildings of the Main Street, the Hall, and the old Bakehouse at the start of Pump Lane. Only in the last decade has the bakery ceased operating.

DOWER HOUSE — Dates from the 16th Century. Has been much altered, as can be seen today by the various blocked windows. It was first altered in 1600. Notice the carved front gates, and how the main street turns abruptly right to squeeze past the house. Originally this was a right of way from Oddo to the village but was made last century into a road, thereby slicing into the grounds of the house.

THE HALL — Built in 1628 by Francis Moore. The gritstone, with which the Hall is built, was brought to Winster on pack horses from Stancliffe Quarries in Darley Dale. The ceilings in the lower rooms had frescoes by West, the successor of Sir Joshua Reynolds as President of the Royal Academy. Later the buildings were occupied by a member of the clergy who objected to the semi-nude nymphs and had them whitewashed over. Today the building has been converted into a hotel. The Hall is also one of the four Lover's Leaps of Derbyshire. According to the legend, the daughter of the house fell in love with the coachman and wanted to marry him. Her parents were concerned because of the poor match, and therefore hurriedly arranged something more suitable. On the eve of the wedding, the daughter and the coachman climbed onto the parapet of the building and, holding hands and swearing everlasting love, they jumped to their deaths. This happened in the mid-18th Century when this kind of demonstration was the vogue. It is said that a white lady haunts the forecourt!

Winster Hall Inn sign

Pancake Races

FOLKLORE

LUNTER ROCKS — On the south-eastern outskirts of the village are the ruins of a building at Lunter Rocks, G.R. SK243604. A footpath from the village goes close to it, en route for Bonsall. According to the story, a murder took place here and the ruins are reputed to be haunted. As a result no Winster children play near there at night.

THE ANGEL INN — The building opposite the Market House was formerly the Angel Inn. Ghost stories are still recalled about the headless bride that was seen here. At the top of the first flight of stairs a woman sat in front of a mirror putting on her make-up, with the door open. While she was doing this she suddenly stopped and stared at the scene in the mirror. Walking up the stairs was a headless bride in her wedding dress. As the bride approached her she screamed and fainted. As to why a headless woman should roam the buildings is not known. There have been other unexplained happenings, such as doors opening and closing and persons walking about when no-one was there.

MORRIS DANCING — During the summer months, visiting teams of Morris Dancers can be seen at several Derbyshire and Peak District villages. In the 1950s Winster had its own team who were in great demand during the summer, even on one occasion going to Cambridge. During Wakes Week at the end of June, Morris Dancing was one of the highlights of the week. Winster had five dances of their own, known as the Morris Dance (Winster version), the Winster Gallop, The Blue Eyed Stranger, the Processional and the Winster Reel. To add to the fun of the proceedings, they have four supernumaries. These characters are the King, the Queen, the Jester and the witch. The Queen was always a youth dressed as a woman, and the parts of both the King and Queen could be played by anyone, as they were not required to dance!

Although no team existed in the mid 1970s, interested people met and in 1978 a new team was started. Today it is very active during the summer months and has revived Winster's rightful place in Derbyshire's traditions. The county of Derbyshire is twinned with the Province of Ascoli Piceno in Italy. The Winster Morris Dancing Team are twinned with the village of Monterubbiano in the Province of Ascoli Piceno. The village has a Flag Waving Team and exchange visits are made.

PANCAKE RACES — Shrove Tuesday has always been a special day on the customs calendar. Being the day before Lent begins, it was usual in olden times to make your confession or 'shriving' as it was called. The word 'shriving' explains the naming of the day, Shrove Tuesday. The day was also an excuse for feasting to eat up any food that could not be eaten during Lent or would not be palatable after Lent.

The origin of the annual Pancake Races at Winster is not known. Nor is the date when they first commenced, but they have been a feature of the village calendar for well over 100 years. Winster is the only Derbyshire village to uphold this custom. The main street is closed to traffic while the races take place. The course is approximately

100 yards long, from the Dower House to the Market House. They commence at 3.00 p.m., and the age of the contestants decides the yardage of each race. The six-year-olds start from about 20 yards from the Market House, and the men from the gates of the Dower House. The races follow strict rules, and special frying pans are used. The pancakes are made from a special recipe so that they are robust and will not disintegrate from the rough punishment; they can even be stood upon without bursting. Naturally, they are not designed for eating but for the rudiments of the race. As you run you must toss the pancake three times. The first three home in each group receive a small prize.

WINSTER PANCAKE RECIPE —

It should be noted that this recipe is not intended to make light pancakes but ones suitable for the rough usage on Race Day.

Ingredients: 1/2 lb. self-raising flour
Pinch of salt
2 eggs
Pint of milk
A noggin of lard.

Method: The eggs should be beaten together before adding the milk and salt. Mix in the flour until fully dispersed and cook mix in a hot frying pan with a little fat.

WINSTER WAKES CAKE -

The return of the Wake never fails to produce a week, at least, of idleness, intoxication, and riot.
(The Claybrook Historian, 1791)

Today several Derbyshire and Peak District villages hold their Wakes Week when social events such as tug of war competitions and Morris Dancing take place. Winster's takes place at the end of June. Originally the Wake was a solemn occasion to celebrate the feast day of the saint to whom the village church is dedicated. The feast day is taken as the day of the death or burial of the saint. The church being dedicated to St. John the Baptist is an exception to the rule. The feast day is June 24th and commemorates his birth, not his death, which was on August 29th. Originally a night of prayer was celebrated in the church, but this was abandoned and the feast day became a village holiday, with feasting and drinking. In the 18th Century it was a whole week of revelry, and special wakes cakes were made for the occasion.

Winster's recipe is as follows:-

Ingredients:
1/2 lb. of plain flour
6 ozs. of butter   1 egg
6 ozs. of castor sugar   1 oz. of currants

Method: Rub flour and butter together, add sugar and currants, mix to a stiff dough with beaten egg, knead a little, roll out and bake in a moderate oven.

OTHER BOOKS BY JOHN N. MERRILL PUBLISHED BY JNM PUBLICATIONS

DAY WALK GUIDES -

SHORT CIRCULAR WALKS IN THE PEAK DISTRICT
LONG CIRCULAR WALKS IN THE PEAK DISTRICT
CIRCULAR WALKS IN WESTERN PEAKLAND
SHORT CIRCULAR WALKS IN THE STAFFORDSHIRE MOORLANDS
SHORT CIRCULAR WALKS AROUND THE TOWNS AND VILLAGES OF THE PEAK DISTRICT
SHORT CIRCULAR WALKS AROUND MATLOCK
SHORT CIRCULAR WALKS IN THE DUKERIES
SHORT CIRCULAR WALKS IN SOUTH YORKSHIRE
SHORT CIRCULAR WALKS AROUND DERBY
SHORT CIRCULAR WALKS AROUND BAKEWELL
SHORT CIRCULAR WALKS AROUND BUXTON
SHORT CIRCULAR WALKS AROUND NOTTINGHAMSHIRE
SHORT CIRCULAR WALKS ON THE NORTHERN MOORS
40 SHORT CIRCULAR PEAK DISTRICT WALKS
SHORT CIRCULAR WALKS IN THE HOPE VALLEY

INSTRUCTION & RECORD -

HIKE TO BE FIT.........................STROLLING WITH JOHN
THE JOHN MERRILL WALK RECORD BOOK

CANAL WALK GUIDES -

VOL ONE — DERBYSHIRE AND NOTTINGHAMSHIRE
VOL TWO — CHESHIRE AND STAFFORDSHIRE
VOL THREE — STAFFORDSHIRE
VOL FOUR — THE CHESHIRE RING
VOL FIVE — LINCOLNSHIRE & NOTTINGHAMSHIRE
VOL SIX — SOUTH YORKSHIRE
VOL SEVEN — THE TRENT & MERSEY CANAL

DAY CHALLENGE WALKS -

JOHN MERRILL'S WHITE PEAK CHALLENGE WALK
JOHN MERRILL'S YORKSHIRE DALES CHALLENGE WALK
JOHN MERRILL'S NORTH YORKSHIRE MOORS CHALLENGE WALK
PEAK DISTRICT END TO END WALKS
THE LITTLE JOHN CHALLENGE WALK
JOHN MERRILL'S LAKELAND CHALLENGE WALK
JOHN MERRILL'S STAFFORDSHIRE MOORLAND CHALLENGE WALK
JOHN MERRILL'S DARK PEAK CHALLENGE WALK

MULTIPLE DAY WALKS -

THE RIVERS' WAY
PEAK DISTRICT HIGH LEVEL ROUTE
PEAK DISTRICT MARATHONS
THE LIMEY WAY
THE PEAKLAND WAY

COAST WALKS -

ISLE OF WIGHT COAST WALK
PEMBROKESHIRE COAST PATH
THE CLEVELAND WAY

HISTORICAL GUIDES -

DERBYSHIRE INNS — an A to Z Guide
HALLS AND CASTLES OF THE PEAK DISTRICT & DERBYSHIRE
TOURING THE PEAK DISTRICT AND DERBYSHIRE BY CAR
DERBYSHIRE FOLKLORE
LOST INDUSTRIES OF DERBYSHIRE
PUNISHMENT IN DERBYSHIRE
CUSTOMS OF THE PEAK DISTRICT AND DERBYSHIRE
WINSTER — A VISITOR'S GUIDE
ARKWRIGHT OF CROMFORD
TALES FROM THE MINES by GEOFFREY CARR
PEAK DISTRICT PLACE NAMES by MARTIN SPRAY

JOHN'S MARATHON WALKS -

TURN RIGHT AT LAND'S END
WITH MUSTARD ON MY BACK
TURN RIGHT AT DEATH VALLEY
EMERALD COAST WALK

COLOUR GUIDES -

THE PEAK DISTRICT............Something to remember her by.

SKETCH BOOKS — by John Creber

NORTH STAFFORDSHIRE SKETCHBOOK

CALENDARS

1989 JOHN MERRILL PEAK DISTRICT WALK A MONTH CALENDAR